All About
Mitosis and Meiosis

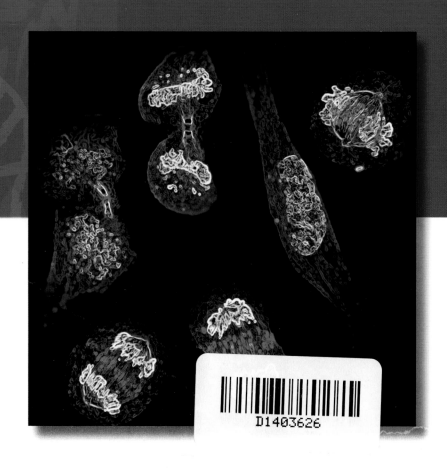

Elizabeth R. C. Cregan

Life Science Readers:
All About Mitosis and Meiosis

Publishing Credits

Editorial Director
Dona Herweck Rice

Associate Editor
Joshua BishopRoby

Editor-in-Chief
Sharon Coan, M.S.Ed.

Creative Director
Lee Aucoin

Illustration Manager
Timothy J. Bradley

Publisher
Rachelle Cracchiolo, M.S.Ed.

Science Contributor
Sally Ride Science™

Science Consultants
Thomas R.Ciccone, B.S., M.A.Ed.,
  Chino Hills High School
Dr. Ronald Edwards,
  DePaul University

Teacher Created Materials

5301 Oceanus Drive
Huntington Beach, CA 92649-1030
http://www.tcmpub.com
ISBN 978-0-7439-0585-5
© 2008 Teacher Created Materials
Printed in China
Nordica.082019.CA21901409

Table of Contents

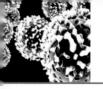

What Are Cells?

All living things, no matter what, are made of cells. Cells are made of **molecules**. Some organisms are just one cell. An **amoeba** is one example. Bacteria are single-celled, too. But some organisms are multicellular. That means they have many cells. Humans are all multicellular. So are animals and plants.

Multicellular things can be made of trillions of cells. The cells work together. They help the organism do many things. They help it eat to create energy. They help it to get rid of waste. They even help it to reproduce, or make new cells. These cells communicate with one another. They do this by exchanging tiny **chemical messages**.

◀ Each petal of each flower of this plant is made of hundreds of thousands of cells.

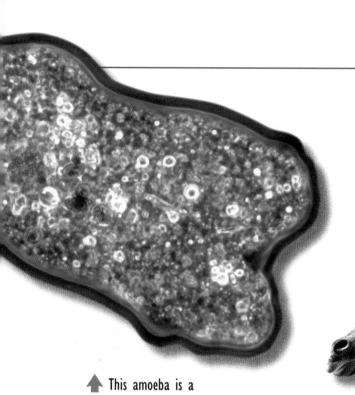

This amoeba is a single-celled animal.

Cells are very busy. Chemical messages move molecules from place to place. It's just like the swirl of action when the bell rings at school. You grab your books and head to your next class. When your cells get a chemical message, they get busy. Thousands of these reactions take place in your body every second.

Are Cells Replaced?

Some cells are replaced every day. Others are almost never replaced. Your skin cells are replaced daily. The cells in your brain are rarely replaced.

Take a Closer Look

Your body is a very busy place. It is busy even when you are sleeping. You are made of 20 to 30 trillion cells. About 25 million new cells are created each second. Most of your cells are very tiny. About 10,000 of these cells can fit on the head of a pin! But nerve cells in a giraffe's neck can be over nine feet long.

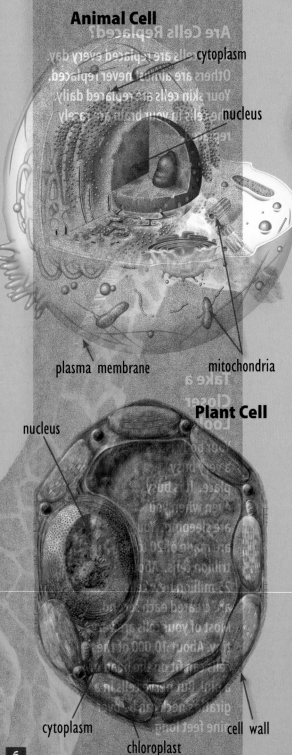

Animal Cell

cytoplasm

nucleus

plasma membrane

mitochondria

Plant Cell

nucleus

cytoplasm

chloroplast

cell wall

Inside the Cell

All cells are alike in some ways. For example, all cells contain **organelles**. Organelles are structures that perform certain jobs in the cell. Each one has a role to play. They all send and receive messages in the cell.

Animal cells are surrounded by a layer of **plasma membrane**. It houses the **cytoplasm**. The cytoplasm makes up half the cell. It processes proteins. **Mitochondria** inside the membrane make up 25 percent of the cytoplasm. They make the energy for the cell. The **nucleus** is inside the membrane, too. It holds the cell's **DNA**. That is the genetic material of the cell.

Plant cells are a bit different. They have a tough cell wall outside the plasma membrane. They have less cytoplasm than animal cells do. Their organelles take up most of the space in the cell. The cell needs the organelles to produce energy.

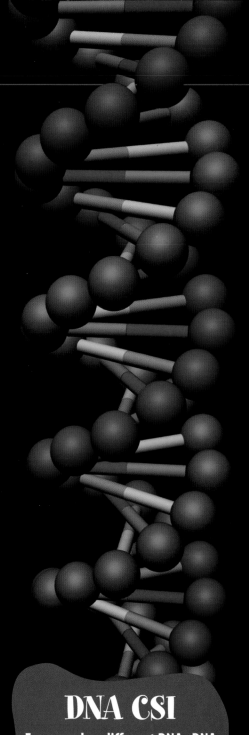

DNA

You probably know that DNA is a recipe for building your body. But how does it work? DNA is in every cell. It is the "brain" behind cell operation.

DNA is a long, stringy molecule. There are instructions along the string called **alleles**. The alleles tell the cell when to make different proteins.

There are two alleles for every **gene**. The cell follows both sets of instructions at the same time. It may make a lot of one protein if both alleles tell it to. Or it might make some of one protein and some of another if the alleles disagree. Whatever the result, the pair of alleles "express" the gene.

DNA CSI

Everyone has different DNA. DNA is even found in blood. That's why police sometimes use it to help them solve crimes.

What Is Mitosis?

The Cell Cycle starts with a period of growth called the **interphase**. It is the time between cell divisions. A cell is in interphase 90 percent of the time. **Mitosis** comes next. That's when the cell divides. Then, the new cells return to interphase.

Cells cannot just split in half. They create complete copies of themselves. The copies include their DNA. Remember, the DNA gives a blueprint for building new cells. The cell must be copied exactly. That is the only way each cell can survive and work properly. This is all part of interphase.

Interphase occurs in three steps. The first step is the G1-phase. The newly formed cell processes all the materials it needs to grow stronger. Then comes the S-phase. The DNA makes a copy of itself. These DNA copies are linked at a point called the **centromere**. Interphase ends with the G2-phase. The cell checks to be sure the newly copied DNA is in order. Now the cell is ready to divide.

Cell division, or mitosis, occurs in five phases. They are the **prophase**, **metaphase**, **anaphase**, **telophase**, and **cytokinesis**. Mitosis takes about two hours to complete.

interphase

prophase

metaphase

anaphase

telophase

cytokinesis

⬆ cell during anaphase

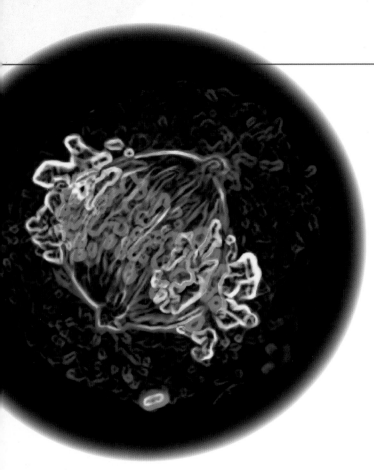

▲ cell during prophase

Prophase

Prophase is the first phase of mitosis. The cell's nuclear membrane disappears first. Then the strands of DNA that paired off during interphase thicken. They become short, stubby rods called **chromatids**. You can look at these under a light microscope. The stubby rods look like tiny Xs. They are attached at the center by the centromere.

Threads

Mitosis comes from the Greek word *mitos*, or thread. Chromosomes look like thread when cells divide.

Signs of Mitosis

Have you ever seen a new shoot poking out of the soil in springtime? That is the result of mitosis. Has your sunburned skin ever peeled? The new skin that grows back is also the result of mitosis.

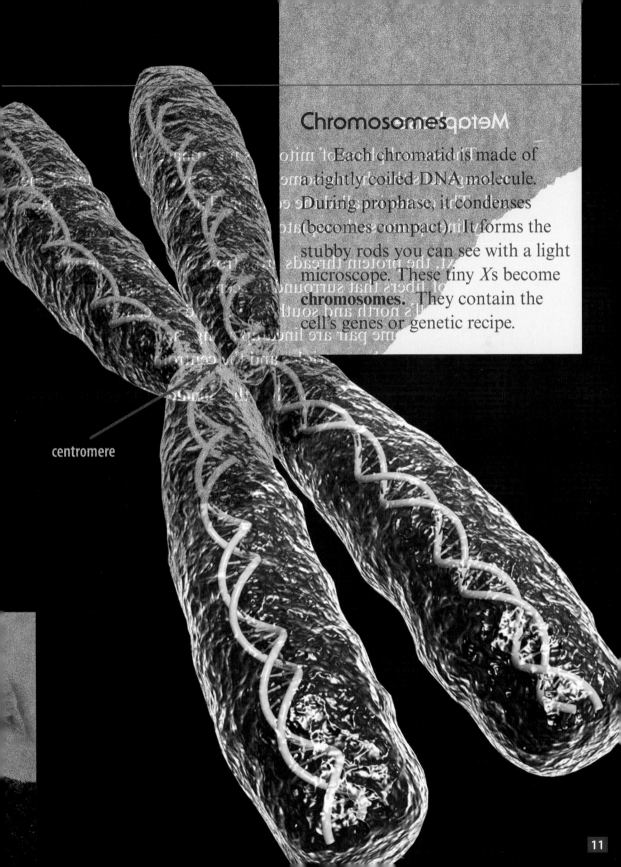

Chromosomes

Each chromatid is made of a tightly coiled DNA molecule. During prophase, it condenses (becomes compact). It forms the stubby rods you can see with a light microscope. These tiny *X*s become **chromosomes.** They contain the cell's genes or genetic recipe.

centromere

Metaphase

The second phase of mitosis is metaphase. A chemical message tells the chromosome pairs to move to the center of the cell. The center is called the equator. The pairs follow orders. They line up across the equator.

Next, the protein threads grow from the **aster**. The aster is made of fibers that surround the centosome. The **centrioles** sit at the cell's north and south poles. And the centromeres on each chromosome pair are lined up along the equator. The threads connect the centrioles and the centromeres.

This new connection is called the **spindle**. The cell is now ready to divide.

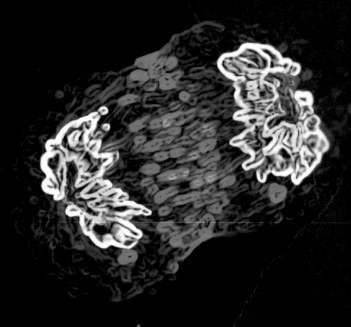

⬆ cell during metaphase

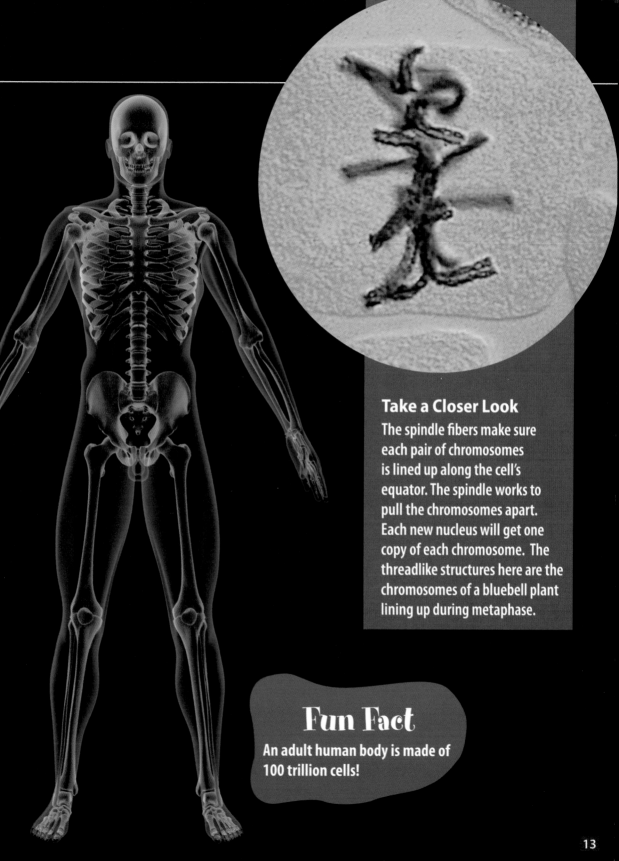

Take a Closer Look

The spindle fibers make sure each pair of chromosomes is lined up along the cell's equator. The spindle works to pull the chromosomes apart. Each new nucleus will get one copy of each chromosome. The threadlike structures here are the chromosomes of a bluebell plant lining up during metaphase.

Fun Fact

An adult human body is made of 100 trillion cells!

cell during anaphase

Take a Closer Look

The spindle fibers make sure each pair of chromosomes

Anaphase

Anaphase is the third phase of mitosis. The cell signals the protein threads of the spindle to lengthen. This makes the cell longer, too. The threads pull the chromosomes toward the poles. Identical sets of chromosomes move toward the poles. Each pole now contains a complete set of chromosomes. When the cell divides, each cell will contain a complete set of the same genetic blueprints.

Madagascar periwinkle

How Honeybees Are Made

Some plants and animals are able to reproduce asexually. To do so, egg cells are duplicated to create offspring. Honeybees reproduce this way.

Amazing Nature

There are substances in nature that can dissolve a spindle before it can pull the chromosomes to a cell's poles. Scientists know about two flowering plants that produce these substances. They are the autumn crocus and the Madagascar periwinkle. They stop cell division and growth. They are used to treat cancer and other diseases.

autumn crocus

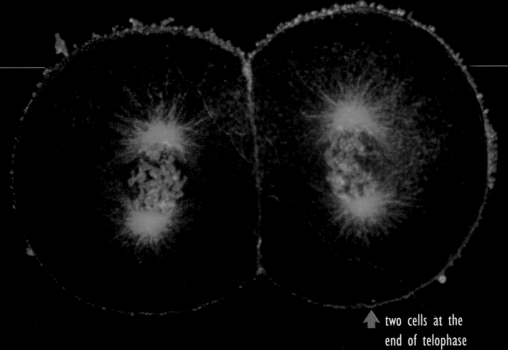

two cells at the end of telophase

Telophase

Mitosis is nearly complete. Telophase is the fourth phase. During telophase, the chromosomes finally arrive at the north and south poles of the cell. They begin to organize themselves into new nuclei. They are no longer visible under the light microscope. A membrane forms around each new nucleus. The spindle fibers begin to disappear. A dent or furrow begins to form down the center of the cell.

The Name Game

When scientists discover a gene, they can name it whatever they want. That is why many have such interesting names. Did you know there is a hedgehog gene? There is even a T-shirt gene. One gene is called dreadlocks. What name would you pick if you discovered a gene?

Making the Small World Large

Light microscopes magnify specimens up to 1,000 times their size. They use a series of lenses to do this. The lenses focus and magnify light that reflects off a specimen. One set of lenses focuses light on the specimen being examined. Another lens gathers the light from the specimen. It focuses the light through a narrow tube. The tube ends in the third lens, or eyepiece. The eyepiece then magnifies the reflected image.

Electron microscopes use electrons instead of light. They use a magnetic field as a lens. It focuses and magnifies the image of a specimen. Electron microscopes can magnify objects two million times!

◀ This scientist is working with an electron microscope.

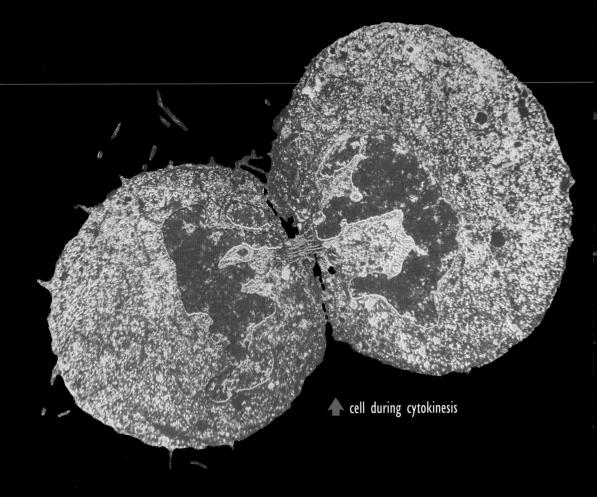

 cell during cytokinesis

Cytokinesis

Cytokinesis is the final phase of mitosis.

Remember the dent in animal cells at the end of telophase? It is actually a fiber ring made of a protein. The protein is called **actin**. This ring pinches the cell into two **daughter cells**.

In plant cells, a cell plate forms down the center of the cell. The cell breaks apart along the cell plate. This forms two daughter cells.

Nearly all cells go through mitosis. It helps cells grow. It helps repair and replace cells. But something very important is missing.

How Do Cells Know?

Have you ever cut your finger? Did new skin form? Skin cells undergo mitosis to create new skin. Exact copies of skin cells are made to replace the ones destroyed by the cut. Growing new cells in this way may be called cell division. It is also known as **asexual reproduction**.

But how do living things create offspring? How do all the kinds of cells that go together to make one living thing get reproduced? How do a mother cat's cells know to grow a kitten and not a puppy? **Meiosis** takes care of that. Meiosis is used in **sexual reproduction**. It is the process living things undergo to reproduce.

What Is Meiosis?

Gila monster

seaweed

fungus

horse and foal

Meiosis is the division of special kinds of cells. It is also called sexual reproduction.

Unlike mitosis, meiosis produces four cells. They are called **gametes**. Each daughter cell contains half the DNA from the parent cell. You can think of gametes as half-cells.

There are many organisms that have cells that undergo meiosis. Seaweed, fungi, and plants do. Animals do, too. Meiosis makes human egg cells in females and sperm cells in males. Flowering plants undergo meiosis. Meiosis makes **megaspore** cells in the flower's ovaries. It makes **microspore** cells in the stamens.

Sperm and egg cells are gametes. ➡ They are made through meiosis.

Many different species use sexual reproduction to create new, unique offspring.

sperm

How Many Chromosomes?

Mitosis creates new cells. In humans, each cell contains all 46 chromosomes. Meiosis creates cells, too. But these cells each have only 23 chromosomes. Then, two sex cells can join together. They create a new organism. It will have a new set of 46 chromosomes that no one has ever had before.

egg

August Weismann

August Weismann was a scientist. He studied cell division of sex cells. He was the first to realize it had to be different than mitosis. If not, how could they end up with just half the total number of chromosomes? He called this special division of sex cells "reduction division."

Meiosis happens in two stages called Meiosis I and Meiosis II. Both stages look a lot like mitosis. At the end of Meiosis I, the original cell has split into two cells. Both cells have DNA, but not all of it. Each cell has two copies of half the original DNA. Later, Meiosis II will split the two full cells into four half-cell gametes. Each gamete has one copy of half the original DNA.

Meiosis I and II each has four stages. They are prophase, metaphase, anaphase, and telophase. They are numbered to match Meiosis I and II.

Before Meiosis I begins, the cell is in interphase. During interphase, chromosomes and organelles are copied. The cell grows. Two pairs of centrioles appear in the cytoplasm.

This is a cell as it appears before meiosis.

During interphase, the chromosomes are copied.

start

Prophase I

Meiosis I starts with prophase I. The centrioles arrange themselves at the north and south poles. Strands of protein shoot out from the centrioles. They begin to form the spindle. The nuclear membrane disappears. The chromosomes shorten and thicken. The spindle grabs the chromosomes.

Metaphase I

Metaphase I is the second stage. Chromosomes get in line on each side of the equator. Half the chromosomes are on one side and half on the other. The chromosomes stay with their copies. The spindle fibers shorten. They pull the chromosomes toward the poles of the cell.

Alphabet Meiosis

One way to think of meiosis is using letters to stand in for the alleles being copied. The original cell might have alleles A, a, B, b, C, c, D, and d. Before meiosis, the genes are copied so the list becomes AAaaBBbbCCccDDdd. Meiosis I ends with one cell having AABBCCDD and the other cell having aabbccdd. Then Meiosis II splits those cells. The AABBCCDD cell splits into ABCD and ABCD. The aabbccdd cell splits into abcd and abcd.

Of course, Meiosis I doesn't pay attention to which allele goes where. It could just as easily create cells with AAbbCCDD and aaBBccdd. They would split to two AbCD cells and two aBcd cells. Each cell would have one of each gene.

In prophase I, centrioles reach out for chromosomes.

In metaphase I, the chromosomes separate into two complete sets.

Anaphase I

The third stage is anaphase I. The spindle fibers continue to shorten. The chromosomes are pulled to the poles of the cell. Because the chromosomes stick with their copies, each side has two copies of half the set. The chromosomes begin to organize themselves into new nuclei.

Telophase I

The process is completed during the last stage. A membrane forms around each new nucleus. A furrow begins to form down the center of the cell. The cell finally splits into two daughter cells. They each contain two copies of half the original DNA.

In anaphase I, the complete sets of chromosomes are pulled toward the centrioles.

In telophase I, the cell divides into two daughter cells.

During cytokinesis, the cells rest.

Meiosis II

The first stage is over. The original cell has split into two daughter cells. They each contain two copies of half the set of chromosomes. The cells rest. This is called **interkinesis**. It is different from interphase because the chromosomes are not copied. Then the cells begin to divide again.

Prophase II

New centrioles form in both daughter cells. They reach out to grab the chromosomes.

Metaphase II

The chromosomes are pulled towards the centrioles. Each centriole only pulls one copy of each chromosome.

Alternation of Generations

Sexual reproduction happens in many organisms. In many kinds of plants, it follows a two-step process. It is called the **alternation of generations**. The plant does the first half of meiosis to make a spore. It contains half the total number of chromosomes found in the rest of the plant's cells. The spores fall off and grow into a prothallus. It looks very different. The prothallus then does the rest of meiosis to make sex cells. They grow into a new plant.

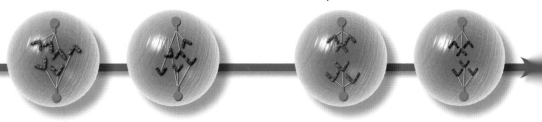

In prophase II, new centrioles reach out for chromosomes.

In metaphase II, the chromosomes separate into half sets.

Anaphase II

The chromosomes pulled to the centrioles get organized. They form into little clumps. Each clump has one copy of half a complete set of chromosomes.

Telophase II

A new nuclear membrane forms around the clumps of chromosomes. Each daughter cell splits into two new cells.

Meiosis II ends with the creation of four daughter cells. Each one has half a copy of DNA.

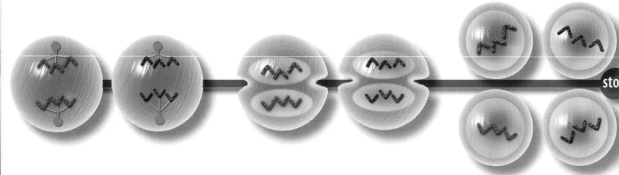

In anaphase II, the half-sets clump together.

In telophase II, the two cells split into four.

Meiosis turns one cell into four gametes.

sto

The Whole Picture

What good are gametes with only half a set of DNA? In animals, a female's gametes are egg cells. A male's gametes are sperm cells. When an egg cell and a sperm cell are combined, together they have a whole set of DNA. The set has some chromosomes from the father and some from the mother.

The new cell uses mitosis to split into two cells, then four, then eight. Over time, the cells can grow into a whole new organism. It will have some traits from its father. It will have other traits from its mother. It will be their child.

Mitosis and meiosis work together and depend on one another. Mitosis helps living things grow new cells and repair damaged cells within themselves. Meiosis helps them produce whole new organisms that are their offspring.

How Many Chromosomes?

Humans have 46 chromosomes. But all living things do not. A mosquito has only six. An onion has 16. And a carp has 104!

two cells during telophase II ➡

In this activity, you will make mobile models of plant and animal cells. Common household materials will be used to represent the structures of plant and animal cells. You will identify and describe the structure and function of organelles.

Materials

- construction paper
- crayons or markers
- tape
- wire clothes hangers (2)
- string or yarn
- plastic wrap
- toothpicks
- self-sealing sandwich bag
- notebook paper and pen or pencil

Procedure

1 Make the following animal cell structures: nucleus, smooth ER, rough ER, mitochondria, vacuole, and lysosome. Use construction paper, crayons, and tape if needed to make the cell structures.

2 Attach the cell structures to the clothes hanger, using the string or yarn.

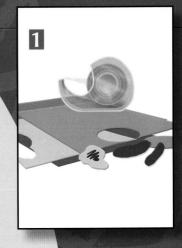

3 Wrap the entire model in plastic wrap to represent the cell membrane.

4 Carefully insert toothpicks into the plastic wrap to represent cilia.

5 Attach a long piece of string or yarn to the plastic wrap or clothes hanger to represent a flagellum.

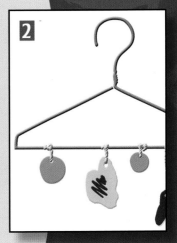

6 Make the following plant cell structures: nucleus, smooth ER, rough ER, mitochondria, chloroplast, vacuole, and lysosome. Use construction paper, crayons, and tape if needed to make the cell structures.

7 Attach the cell structures to the second clothes hanger, using the string or yarn.

8 Wrap the entire model in plastic wrap to represent the cell membrane.

9 Cover the plastic wrap with the self-sealing sandwich bag to represent the cell wall.

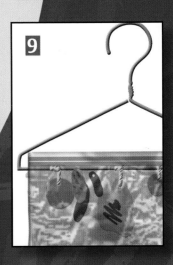

10 On a sheet of notebook paper, list all the parts of the cells used in the cell models. Describe the design of your cell parts. The descriptions should explain how your cell parts work together.

Glossary

actin—a protein that forms at the end of telophase; pinches the animal cells into two daughter cells

alternation of generations—a two-step process of sexual reproduction in the life cycle of plants

allele—instructions in DNA that tell the cell when to make different proteins

amoeba—a single-celled organism

anaphase—the phase of cell division in which the spindle fibers shorten to pull chromosomes to the poles of the cell

asexual reproduction—a form of reproduction that does not involve meiosis, gamete formation, or fertilization

aster—raylike fibers that surround the centrosome during mitosis

centriole—a structure that appears during metaphase that act as the starting point for the protein strands that form the spindle

centromere—the spot joining copied strands of DNA

chemical messages—how cells communicate and molecules move from place to place

chloroplasts—organelles in plant cells that help process carbon dioxide and produce oxygen

chromatid—DNA that has thickened to form short, stubby rods during prophase

chromosome—a structure made of a coiled DNA molecule that appears during mitosis and meiosis

cytokinesis—the final phase of cell division in which the original cell is split to form two new cells

cytoplasm—contents of a cell contained within the plasma membrane

daughter cell—either of the two identical cells that form when a cell divides

DNA—deoxyribonucleic acid; stores the genetic material in a cell's nucleus

gamete—a cell connected with sexual reproduction

gene—a section of DNA that contains the genetic blueprint for a specific trait of an organism

interkinesis—the abbreviated interphase that occurs between meiosis I and II

interphase—a period of cell growth

megaspore—the larger of two types of spores that give rise to a female gametophyte

meiosis—the process of cell division, called reduction division or sexual reproduction

metaphase—phase of cell division in which the chromosome pairs move to the equator of the cell

microspore—the smaller of two types of spores that give rise to a male gametophyte

mitochondria—an organelle that produces a cell's energy

mitosis—the process of cell division or asexual reproduction

molecule—the simplest unit of a chemical substance, usually a group of two or more atoms

nucleus—the organelle containing DNA

organelle—a differentiated structure within a cell, such as a mitochondrion, vacuole, or chloroplast, that performs a specific function

plasma membrane—the membrane surrounding the cytoplasm of animal cells

prophase—the first phase of mitosis in which the chromosomes appear

sexual reproduction—reproduction involving the union or fusion of a male and a female gamete

spindle—tiny fibers seen in cell division

telophase—the phase of cell division in which a membrane forms around each new nucleus, the spindle fiber begin to disappear, and a furrow begins to form down the center of the cell

Index

actin, 18

amoeba, 4–5, 19

anaphase, 9, 14, 22, 24, 26

anaphase I, 24

anaphase II, 26

asexual reproduction, 15, 19

aster, 12

alternation of generations, 24

autumn crocus, 14

bacteria, 4

cell growth, 22

centriole, 12, 22–23

centromere, 8, 10, 12

chemical messages, 4–5, 12

chromatid, 10–11

chromosome, 10–16, 21-27

cytokinesis, 9, 18, 24

cytoplasm, 6, 22

daughter cells, 18, 20, 24–26

DNA, 6–11, 20–27

electron microscope, 17

gametes, 20, 22, 26–27

gene, 7, 11, 26–27

inside the cell, 6–7

interkinesis, 25

interphase, 8–10, 22, 25

light microscope, 10–11, 16–17

Madagascar periwinkle, 15

megaspore, 20

meiosis, 20–27

meiosis I, 22, 25

meiosis II, 26–27

metaphase, 9, 12–13, 22–23, 25

metaphase I, 23

metaphase II, 25

microspore, 20

mitochondria, 6, 28–29

mitosis, 8–19, 21–23, 26–27

molecules, 4–5, 11

nucleus, 6–7, 13, 16–24

organelles, 6, 22, 28

plasma membrane, 6

prophase, 9–11, 22–23, 25

prophase I, 23

prophase II, 25

prothallus, 25

sexual reproduction, 19–20, 25

spindle, 12–16, 23–25

telophase, 9, 16–18, 24, 26–27

telophase I, 24–25

telophase II, 26

Weismann, August, 21

Sally Ride Science™ is an innovative content company dedicated to fueling young people's interests in science. Our publications and programs provide opportunities for students and teachers to explore the captivating world of science—from astrobiology to zoology. We bring science to life and show young people that science is creative, collaborative, fascinating, and fun.